STATISTICS ABOUT U.S. SPECIAL OPS, PAST AND PRESENT

by **Kirsten W. Larson**

Consultant:
Raymond L. Puffer, PhD
Historian, Retired
Edwards Air Force Base History Office

CAPSTONE PRESS
a capstone imprint

Connect is published by Capstone Press,
1710 Roe Crest Drive, North Mankato, Minnesota 56003
www.mycapstone.com

Library of Congress Cataloging-in-Publication Data
Names: Larson, Kirsten W., author.
Title: Statistics about U.S. special ops, past and present / by Kirsten W.
    Larson.
Description: North Mankato, Minnesota: Capstone Press, [2017] | Series:
    Connect. U.S. special ops | Includes bibliographical references and index.
Identifiers: LCCN 2015043650 | ISBN 9781515718529 (library binding) |
    ISBN 9781515718550 (eBook PDF)
Subjects: LCSH: Special forces (Military science)—Juvenile literature. |
    Special operations (Military science)—United States—History—Juvenile
    literature.
Classification: LCC UA34.S64 L37 2017 | DDC 356/.160973021—dc23
LC record available at http://lccn.loc.gov/2015043650

Editorial Credits
Brenda Haugen, editor; Steve Mead, designer;
Jo Miller, media researcher; Katy LaVigne, production specialist

Photo Credits
Corbis: Don Trofani, 22, 32, Medford Historical Society Collection, 35 (top); Getty
Images, 42; Newscom: akg-images, 36, dpa/picture-alliance, 12, Everett Collection, 38,
Picture History/E. & H.T. Anthony, 33; Photo by: Air National Guard Photographer,
TSgt Culeen Shaffer, 31 (top); Shutterstock: Militarist, 23 (bottom), Oleg Zabielin, 6, 7
(top and middle), Przemek Tokar, 7 (bottom), Vartanov Anatoly, 23 (top and middle);
The Art Archive at Art Resource, N.Y., 34; U.S. Air Force photo by Senior Airman
Julianne Showalter, 25 (bottom), Senior Airman Xavier Lockley, 25 (top), Staff Sgt.
Jonathan Snyder, 5; U.S. Army photo by Pfc. Benjamin Tuck, 20, Sgt. Cody Barber,
11th Public Affairs Detachment, 31 (bottom), Sgt. Jason Carter, 44, Sgt. Jessi Ann
McCormick, 40, Spc. Jesse LaMorte / Special Operations Task Force - South, 41, Spc.
Steven Hitchcock, cover, Spc. Steven K. Young, 8, Staff Sgt. John Bainter, 25 (middle),
Staff Sgt. Teddy Wade, 10, Visual Information Specialist Adam Sanders, 27 (top); U.S.
Marine Corps photo by 2nd Lt Scott Villiard, 26, Cpl. Kyle McNally, 18, Cpl. Matthew
Manning, 31 (middle); U.S. Naval History & Heritage Command, 35 (bottom); U.S.
Navy photo by MC1 Elisandro T. Diaz, 27 (bottom), MC3 Blake Midnight, 14, Mr. Paul
Farley, 29 (top), PHC Andrew McKaskle, 28, PO1 Kathryn Whittenberger, 29 (bottom);
Wikimedia: AFSOC, 16

Design Elements
Shutterstock: Aekkaphob, angel digital, Artur. B, B Sanja, Benguhan, ducu59us,
EtoileArk, evgdemidova, Evgeniia Speshneva, Ficus777, Jan Zabsky, Kanate, kasha_
malasha, MSF, 11, MSG64, MSSA, Nik Merkulov, Oleg Zabielin, oorka, Ozger Sarikaya,
Pyty, Rashad Ashurov, sn4ke, springart, Studioicon, super1973, Tomacco, Victor
Metelskiy

Printed and bound in Canada.
009649F16

TABLE OF CONTENTS

CHAPTER 1

FEW BUT DEADLY

Special operations groups of the United States military differ from other soldiers in many ways. Special ops consist of only the best of the best from a group that volunteers for the job. Then candidates train for months. Their training weeds out all but the toughest and smartest fighters.

Special forces members also fight differently than soldiers from earlier times. In the Civil War (1861–1865) or World War II (1939–1945), soldiers tried to win big battles. They often needed more men and firepower to win. Special ops groups work in small teams or alone. They often work in enemy areas for days or months. They gather information about a place or an enemy's plans, weapons, and forces. They rescue prisoners or people who are hurt. They **raid** hideouts to capture **terrorists** and learn more about their plans. Sometimes they train fighters in other countries. All of this is called irregular warfare.

The U.S. military uses special ops now more than ever. Following the terrorist attacks of September 11, 2001, the number of special ops forces grew. The groups have played major roles in the wars in Iraq and Afghanistan. Though special ops remains a small part of the U.S. military, statistics show they have a big impact both in the past and today.

The Growth of U.S. Special Ops Since 9/11

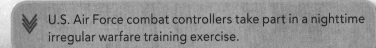

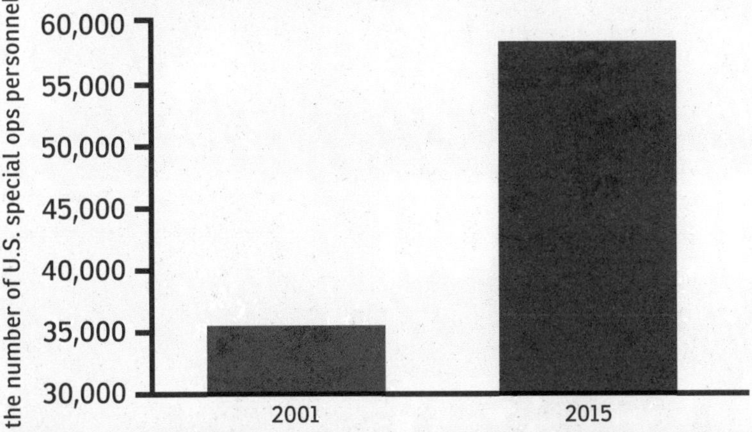
the number of U.S. special ops personnel
60,000
55,000
50,000
45,000
40,000
35,000
30,000
2001
2015

U.S. Air Force combat controllers take part in a nighttime irregular warfare training exercise.

raid—a sudden, surprise attack on a place

terrorist—someone who uses violence and threats to frighten people

GREEN BERETS, RANGER REGIMENT, AND DELTA FORCE

1,000,000
the number of soldiers serving in the U.S. Army

300 TO 350
the number of soldiers in Delta Force, the Army's most **elite** and secret special ops unit

3,500
the number of men serving in the 75th Ranger Regiment. This special ops group can be anywhere around the world in 18 hours, ready to invade or carry out raids.

10,000 TO 20,000
the number of U.S. Army Special Forces, also known by their nickname, Green Berets. The Green Berets is an elite group focused on missions, such as stopping terrorists and training foreign militaries.

elite—among the very best

intelligence—secret information about an enemy's plans or actions

tactic—a plan for fighting a battle

NAVY SEALS

330,000
the number of men and women serving in the U.S. Navy

3,000
the number of Navy SEALs (Sea, Air, Land), the Navy's special ops unit, which performs quick attacks, gathers **intelligence**, and other missions

AIR FORCE SPECIAL TACTICS

310,000
the number of men and women serving in the U.S. Air Force

1,000
the number of Special **Tactics** Airmen, including weathermen, controllers, and rescue crews, who work deep behind enemy lines

MARINE SPECIAL OPERATIONS

200,000
the number of men and women serving in the U.S. Marine Corps

960
the number of Marine Corps Raiders, experts in small strikes, gathering intelligence, and other missions

★ ★ ☆ ☆ ☆ ☆ ☆ ☆

CHAPTER 2

MEET THE OPERATORS

GREEN BERETS

The Army created the Army Special Forces in 1952. Members are called Green Berets because of the caps they wear. Army leaders wanted a unit that, among other duties, could work with local **resistance** groups. Special **agents** had done this in Europe and Asia during World War II. For example, agents had parachuted into France to help the French resistance fight the Germans. After World War II, the Green Berets continued this work.

The Green Berets play a big role in today's wars. In Afghanistan they rid villages of terrorists. Then they form relationships with local people. They also train local police forces.

When they are on secret missions, Green Berets do not wear uniforms. They don't want to be identified as Green Berets. Instead they blend in with local people. In Afghanistan they grow beards like Arab men do.

resistance—a group that fights back against those in control of a conquered country; resistance members often operate in secret

agent—a spy

GREEN BERET STATS

3 97% failed — the percentage of candidates who pass the Qualification Course, which lasts more than a year

7 the height in feet (2.1 meters) of the wall Green Berets must scale as part of a 2-mile (3.2-kilometer) obstacle course

12 the number of men in a Green Beret team. Each team has an officer, a warrant officer, and 10 sergeants with specialties such as medicine or weapons. The teams can split into smaller groups of six.

20 the minimum age to join the Green Berets

50 the number of meters candidates must swim during training wearing boots

$1,000 the extra pay Green Berets receive each month for special skills, such as parachuting, diving, and speaking foreign languages

GREEN BERET TRAINING

Preparation Course: 25 days of physical fitness and land navigation ❯ Assessment and Selection: 19 days physical and mental fitness ❯ Qualification or "Q" Course: about 63 weeks

PHASE 1
six weeks orientation and history of Green Berets

PHASE 2
13 weeks marksmanship, working as a small unit, mock-fighting groups trying to take over governments, **urban** operations, survival, avoiding capture, resistance, and escape training

PHASE 3
14 to 16 weeks training in the soldier's operations specialty, such as weapons, engineering, medical training, or communications

PHASE 4
four weeks training exercise involving the made-up country of Pineland

PHASE 5
24 weeks language and cultural training

75TH RANGER REGIMENT

Army Rangers fought in World War II, the Korean War (1950–1953), and the Vietnam War (1959–1975). But after each war, the Army deactivated the groups. This changed in 1974 when the Army formed the first ongoing Ranger **battalions.** The Army needed men with the skills of the Rangers.

"Rangers Lead the Way" is the Rangers' motto. They often are the first to fight. Today they fight alongside other special forces, such as Green Berets and Navy SEALs. They also work with other U.S. Army and foreign military troops. One of their jobs is to capture or kill terrorists through small attacks.

Rangers have served in the Middle East since 2001. They usually serve four months before returning to the United States.

U.S. Army Rangers go through training to clear buildings of threats.

battalion—a group of about 300 to 1,000 soldiers

RANGER STATS

4

the number of Ranger battalions, three based in Georgia and one in Washington state

35

the weight in pounds (16 kilograms) of a soldier's backpack on a 12-mile (19.3-km) hike. The training hike must be completed in three hours or less.

40

the number of minutes soldiers have to finish a 5-mile (8-km) run at Ranger School

75

the percentage of soldiers who complete the two-month Ranger School

20

the hours each day soldiers may train during Ranger School

350

the number of enemies one battalion of Rangers killed in Iraq in just four months of the Iraq War (2003–2011)

750

the number of prisoners that same battalion took, along with weapons, explosives, and documents

DELTA FORCE

The U.S. Army formed Delta Force in 1977. The rise of terrorism in the late 1970s helped lead to the group's birth. Palestinians took Israeli athletes **hostage** and killed almost all of them during the 1972 Summer Olympics in Munich, Germany. Four years later Palestinians took Israelis prisoner at an airport in Uganda. That led many European countries to form hostage rescue groups. The United States formed Delta Force.

Most of Delta Force's work is secret. Sometimes reports about their missions leak out. In 2009 Delta Force worked with Navy SEALs in eastern Afghanistan to fight members of the Taliban. In 2013 Delta Force sneaked into Tripoli, Libya. They arrested an al-Qaeda terrorist in front of his house. He was accused of participating in the bombing of two U.S. embassies in 1998.

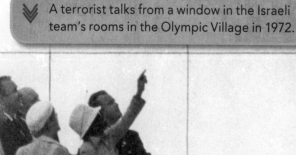

A terrorist talks from a window in the Israeli team's rooms in the Olympic Village in 1972.

hostage—a person held against his or her will

DELTA FORCE STATS

4 TO 6 the number of men on a Delta Force team

5 the length in hours of the interview that candidates must complete at the end of selection and training

10 the percentage of soldiers who pass selection and training and enter the operators course

18 the number of miles (29 km) that soldiers must be able to march in 10 hours

21 the minimum age to join Delta Force

35 the number of push-ups soldiers must do in a minute

37 the number of sit-ups soldiers must do in a minute

100 the estimated number of people who try out for Delta Force each year

DELTA FORCE TRAINING

PHASE 1

Selection and Assessment: three to four weeks physical fitness, land navigation, wilderness survival, interviews

PHASE 2

Operators Course: six months hostage rescue, rappelling down thick ropes from helicopters, getting behind enemy lines, conducting raids, marksmanship, underwater diving

Total training can last up to two years.

U.S. NAVY SEALS

The first two SEAL teams were formed in 1962 during the Vietnam War. During the war the United States fought alongside the South Vietnamese against the North Vietnamese. Navy SEALs ambushed the North Vietnamese and gathered information. SEALs also trained the South Vietnamese.

Many of the first SEALs had served on **demolition** teams. These groups cleared explosives from beaches in Europe and Asia during World War II, allowing soldiers to land safely.

Today SEALs travel by land, air, or sea. They have been a part of the wars in Iraq and Afghanistan. They carry out highly dangerous, secret operations. They were sent on the mission to get Osama bin Laden, the mastermind of the 9/11 terrorist attacks. SEALs also have killed terrorists in Somalia. They train foreign armies and sometimes serve as spies.

SEALs save hostages too. Near Somalia SEALs freed an American ship captain who was being held by a group of pirates in 2009. A team of SEALs positioned themselves on a nearby Navy ship. SEAL snipers pointed their guns at the pirates and waited. When they had clear shots, the snipers fired and killed three pirates. The ship captain was saved.

U.S. NAVY SEALS STATS

1 the number of SEAL Delivery Vehicle Teams, which can deliver SEALs to and from their missions

9 the number of active duty SEAL teams. There are also two reserve teams.

4 the number of SEAL support teams, such as supply, **intelligence**, and cultural engagement

10 the number of pull-ups a SEAL must finish in two minutes

20 TO 25 the percentage of candidates who complete SEAL training

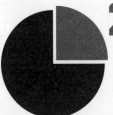

28 the oldest a sailor can be when applying to the SEALs unless he has special permission

1,000 the number of men who enter SEAL training each year

U.S. NAVY SEALS TRAINING

63 WEEKS TOTAL

Special Warfare Prep School: five to nine weeks physical fitness **>** Orientation for Basic Underwater Demolition/SEAL (BUD/S): three weeks physical fitness, teamwork, perseverance **>** BUD/S

PHASE 1

seven weeks of physical fitness; making surveys of the physical features of oceans, seas, and coastal areas; during the third week, candidates are tested on their physical and mental toughness under stressful conditions, including no more than four hours of sleep a night

PHASE 2

seven weeks of combat diving and swimming

PHASE 3

seven weeks of land warfare, training including basic weapons, demolition, land navigation, patrolling, rappelling, marksmanship, and small-unit tactics

SEAL Qualification Training lasts about 30 weeks and includes many skills already practiced. They learn cold weather and medical skills and land navigation. Before SEALs finish, they complete a survival, evasion, resistance, and escape course and attend jump school.

demolition—the act of destroying something

intelligence—secret information about an enemy's plans or actions

U.S. Air Force special operators train in all kinds of conditions.

AIR FORCE SPECIAL TACTICS

Today's U.S. Air Force uses special aircraft and highly trained airmen for special ops. The Air Force's elite ground troops are the Special Tactics Airmen. Special Tactics Airmen work with Navy SEALs, Green Berets, and other special ops teams on the ground. The Airmen often are the only Air Force people with the group. Air Force weathermen parachute into foggy areas of Afghanistan to observe the weather. They make sure aircraft can land safely. Combat controllers climb down ropes from helicopters to take over airfields. They also lead pilots to enemy targets. When soldiers or airmen are hurt and trapped, pararescuemen fly to the scene. They give medical care and fly the injured to safety.

AIR FORCE STATS

2 the number of years it can take to complete Special Tactics training. Training is different for each career field but may include climbing down ropes from helicopters, handling boats, survival skills, combat, shooting, demolition, and parachuting.

2 the number of pararescuemen who work together. They fly to crash sites in helicopters.

20 the percentage of volunteers who pass all training to become Special Tactics Airmen

25 the length in meters that Special Tactics Airmen must swim underwater, twice

50 the weight in pounds (22.7 kg) of the backpack special weathermen and combat controllers must carry on a 3-mile (4.8-km) march

MARINE SPECIAL OPS

The U.S. Marine Corps officially formed its special forces in 2006. Yet Marines have been involved in special operations for many years. From 1942 to 1944, the Raiders worked in the Pacific, where they paved way for larger U.S. military forces. Raiders made surprise attacks, spending weeks behind enemy lines. In June 2015 U.S. Marine Corps Forces Special Operations Command (MARSOC) renamed itself Marine Raiders after the historic World War II group. Today's Marine Corps Raiders perform both quick strikes and irregular warfare.

A special operations Marine waits to ambush the enemy in Afghanistan in 2012.

MARINE RAIDER STATS

3
the number of Marine Raider battalions

7
the number of Medals of Honor won by the Marine Raiders in World War II; the Medal of Honor is the nation's highest military honor.

9
the number of months of experience a Marine must have before applying to become a Raider

10
the number of characteristics a Marine Raider needs

- integrity
- effective intelligence
- physical ability
- adaptability
- initiative
- dependability
- determination
- teamwork
- interpersonal skills
- stress tolerance

12
the number of miles (19.3 km) a Marine Raider trainee must be able to march with a 45-pound (20.4-kg) pack in three hours

14
the number of men on a Raider team

48
the number of Raider teams in 2015

328
the number of yards (300 m) a Marine trainee must be able to swim, fully dressed

7,710
the number of Marines who served in the Marine Raiders during World War II

MARINE RAIDER TRAINING

Assessment and Selection

PHASE 1
21 days of swimming, marching with heavy backpacks, and treading water

PHASE 2
LENGTH IS SECRET

Individual Training Course: nine months of marksmanship, survival, medical and communications skills, information, amphibious and small-unit tactics, and urban combat

★ ★ ★ ☆ ☆ ☆ ☆ ☆

CHAPTER 3

WOMEN IN SPECIAL OPS

Until 2016 women were barred from special operator positions. This meant they could not be Green Berets, Rangers, SEALs, Delta Force, Special Tactics Airmen, or Night Stalkers.

Still women have worked in special ops in many ways. They have served as pilots, navigators, intelligence analysts, and cultural liaisons. For example, Lieutenant Colonel Allison Black, an AC-130H gunship navigator with Air Force Special Operations Command, has been nicknamed "The Angel of Death." In 2001 she and her crew fired from their gunship at Taliban and al-Qaeda locations in Afghanistan. She now leads a Special Operations **squadron** at Hurlburt Field, Florida.

squadron—the basic fighting unit of the U.S. Air Force

Women with the Navy SEALs cultural engagement team also have worked with Muslim women and children in Afghanistan. Wearing Muslim headscarves along with their Navy uniforms, the American women question local women about enemy activities. They also talk with local women to help build good relationships.

2 the number of women who graduated from U.S. Army Ranger school in August 2015

20 the percentage of U.S. Air Force special ops positions held by women in 2015

FEMALE NIGHT STALKERS

In June 2013 the Army's special ops "Night Stalkers" began accepting female helicopter pilots. The Night Stalkers, known as the 160th Special Operations Aviation Regiment, are the Army's elite group of special operations helicopter pilots. They can reach their targets anywhere in the world within 30 seconds of the required time. Since 2001 the Night Stalkers have supported the U.S. wars in the Middle East. Night Stalkers strike targets and deliver special operators to and from their missions, often at night and under fire. Training takes about two years. There are four Night Stalker battalions, two at Fort Campbell, Kentucky, one at Hunter Army Airfield, Georgia, and one at Fort Lewis, Washington.

DECEMBER 3, 2015 the date Defense Secretary Ashton Carter decided to open all combat jobs to women, including special ops ground troops. As long as they qualify and meet the standards, women could become Navy SEALs and Green Berets, for example.

APRIL 1, 2016 the date special ops began to include women in selection and training

★ ★ ★ ★ ☆ ☆ ☆ ☆
SPECIAL OPS WEAPONS

Special ops soldiers use whatever weapons it takes to get the job done, a practice that dates back to colonial times. During the French and Indian War (1754–1763), the British fought both the French and American Indians for control of the interior of what would later become the United States. The Rangers, who were created during this time, adopted American Indian fighting techniques, such as hiding in the brush. They also carried hatchets or tomahawks used by American Indians.

Sometimes special ops groups modify existing weapons to suit their needs. Colonial Rangers sawed off about 11 inches (28 centimeters) from the Brown Bess Musket, making it lighter and easier to carry. In other cases, special ops groups have special weapons developed for them. U.S. Special Operations Command had the Mark 23 pistol made for use by special ops groups from all military branches.

$1,186

10
the number of rounds per minute Union Sharpshooters could fire during the U.S. Civil War with their Sharps rifles. The Sharpshooters were a special ops group from the Northern states, which was often sent ahead of other soldiers during their fight against the Southern states.

the cost of each Mark 23 pistol in 1995

A Navy SEAL knife that was carried during the raid to get Osama bin Laden sold at auction for $35,400. The money went to aid the family of a SEAL Team Six member killed in a training accident.

SPECIAL OPS GUNS

M4 LIGHT, AUTOMATIC RIFLE

 6.11 pounds (2.8 kg)

6.11 pounds (2.8 kg)

700 to 950 rounds per minute

600-meter range

M39 ENHANCED MARKSMANSHIP RIFLE

16.5 pounds (7.5 kg)

60 rounds per minute

780-meter range

M9 PISTOL

2.6 pounds (1.2 kg) loaded

15 rounds

50-meter range

MK11 SNIPER RIFLE

15.2 pounds (7 kg) empty

750 rounds per minute

1,400-meter range

MP5 SUBMACHINE GUN

6.8 pounds (3 kg)

800 rounds per minute

25–100-meter range

MARK 23 PISTOL

4.67 pounds (2 kg) loaded and with a **suppressor**

12 rounds

50-meter range

suppressor—a device on the barrel of a gun that reduces the noise when the gun is fired

★ ★ ★ ★ ★ ☆ ☆ ☆

CHAPTER 5

SPECIAL OPS VEHICLES

Today special ops groups use a variety of vehicles for reconnaissance and operations. Watercraft, airplanes, and helicopters help special operators gather information or sneak behind enemy lines. On land, special ops use specially armored Humvees, which are fast and stealthy. A 12-man Delta Force team uses four of these vehicles to patrol deep behind enemy lines, often travelling 275 miles (442 km) or more. Rangers use smaller Land Rover-type vehicles. They also use all-terrain vehicles (ATVs) and even motorcycles.

Special ops used airplanes for the first time during World War II. In Europe B-24 Liberators dropped secret agents called "Joes" into Nazi-occupied France. The planes were modified for the job. They were painted black so people manning searchlights could not spot the aircraft at night. When a plane neared a drop zone, the crew called to the ground with special radios. The space on the underside of the plane that usually held a gunner was removed. Instead a "Joe hole" was created so Joes could parachute from the planes.

Today the Air Force special ops rely on many different aircraft. Some, such as the U-28A, are used to gather intelligence. Others, such as the CV-22 Osprey, drop off troops behind enemy lines. The AC-130-U Spooky Gunship, a highly modified C-130, hits enemy targets. The gunship can hit a truck in the middle of a city.

SPECIAL OPS VEHICLES

U-28A

JOB: intelligence, surveillance, reconnaissance

CREW MEMBERS: 4   **ENGINE:** 1

SPEED: 220 knots (253 miles per hour) (407 km per hour) cruising speed

MAXIMUM OPERATING ALTITUDE: 30,000 feet (9,144 m)

IN SERVICE: 28

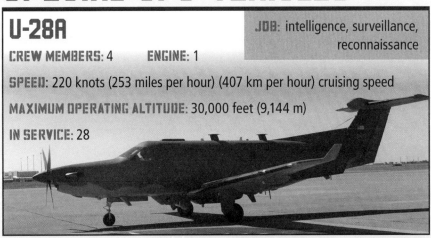

CV-22 OSPREY

JOB: transport, resupply

CREW MEMBERS: 6

ENGINES: 2

SPEED: 241 knots (277 mph) (446 kmph) cruising speed

MAXIMUM OPERATING ALTITUDE: 25,000 feet (7,620 m)

WEAPONS: One .50-caliber machine gun

IN SERVICE: 33

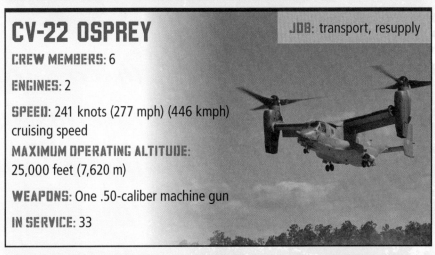

AC-130-U SPOOKY GUNSHIP

JOB: support troops on the battlefield, reconnaissance

CREW MEMBERS: 13

ENGINES: 4

SPEED: 261 knots (300 mph) (483 kmph) cruising speed

MAXIMUM OPERATING ALTITUDE: 25,000 feet (7,620 m)

WEAPONS: 40mm, and 105mm cannons, and 25mm Gatling gun

IN SERVICE: 17

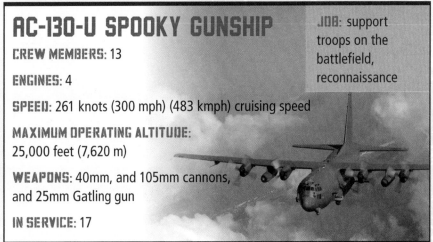

HELICOPTERS

The Army's Night Stalkers work with special ops teams from all military services. They fly many different types of helicopters.

184

the number of helicopters the Night Stalkers operated in 2011

2

the number of different types of Black Hawks used by the Night Stalkers. The MH-60K and MH-60L transport special operators, and the MH-60L is a gunship.

MH-6 LITTLE BIRD

CREW: 2 (pilot and co-pilot)

CAPACITY: 6 passengers

LENGTH: 32.6 feet (9.9 m)

HEIGHT: 9.8 feet (3 m)

SPEED: 135 knots (155 mph) (250 kmph)

RANGE: 267 (430 km) miles at 5,000 feet (1,524 m)

GUNS: one 30mm M-230 chain gun; two .50-caliber GAU-19 Gatling guns or two 7.62mm M-134 mini-guns

ROCKETS: two 70mm Hydra 70 rocket pods

MISSILES: two TOW anti tank missiles or Stinger anti-air missiles

MH-47 CHINOOK

JOB: deliver special ops forces, air attacks, resupply

CREW: 3 (pilot, co-pilot, flight engineer)

CAPACITY: 33 to 55 troops or 28,000 pounds (12,701 kg) of cargo

LENGTH: 98.8 feet (30.1 m)

HEIGHT: 9.8 feet (3 m)

SPEED: 130 knots (150 mph) (241 kmph) cruising speed

RANGE: 460 miles

MH-60 BLACK HAWK

JOB: deliver special ops forces, resupply, direct action, search and rescue

SPEED: 120 knots (138 mph) (222 kmph)

RANGE: 518 miles (834 km)

WATERCRAFT

Special ops forces use rafts, submersibles, and boats to deliver troops and to spy on enemies. During World War II, the Navy's Underwater Demolition Teams used small rafts known as "mattresses" in the Pacific. The rafts helped swimmers get close to islands. Then they could roll off the raft and swim the rest of the way.

During the Vietnam War, the Navy Mobile Riverine Force patrolled the rivers using a number of watercraft. They kept enemies from getting supplies. They also delivered Navy SEALs, who destroyed enemy supplies and bases. The heavily armed boats often attacked enemies along the water's edge. Today the SEALs use both boats and submersibles to reach their targets.

SEAL DELIVERY VEHICLE

JOB: underwater delivery of SEAL teams to and from missions

a wet submersible (crew and SEALs must wear diving equipment)

CREW: 2 (pilot and co-pilot)

CAPACITY: fully equipped SEAL team

POWER: silver-zinc battery

LENGTH: 21 feet (6.4 m)

DEPLOYMENT: They are typically launched from a dry deck shelter on a submarine. They also can be launched from an amphibious carrier or dropped by aircraft (without a crew).

DRY DECK SHELTER

LENGTH: about 40 feet (12.2 m)

WIDTH: about 10 feet (3 m)

HEIGHT: about 10 feet (3 m)

WEIGHT: 65,000 pounds (29,484 kg)

VOLUME: 3,705 cubic feet (105 cubic meters)

MARK V SPECIAL OPERATIONS CRAFT

JOB: delivery of SEAL teams to and from missions when the risk is low to medium

CREW: 5

CAPACITY: 16 fully equipped SEALs

LENGTH: 82 feet (25 m)

BEAM: 17.5 feet (5.3 m)

WEIGHT: 57 tons (52 metric tons)

SPEED: 50 knots (58 mph) (93 kmph)

FACT

The Green Berets sometimes use two-person kayaks to glide silently through water.

★★★★★★☆☆
SPECIAL OPS GEAR

Special ops troops use special gear to help them sneak up on their enemies. Night vision goggles (NVGs) help them see in very little light. Night Stalker pilots use aviation NVGs when they are flying under the cover of darkness. On the ground SEALs and other special ops teams wear NVGs to sneak into enemy territory. SEALs used four-tube NVGs, for example, on the raid to get Osama bin Laden.

When parachuting into enemy territory, troops use steerable parachutes. Aircraft drop jumpers at high altitudes. Jumpers can steer their parachutes to landing sites 30 miles (47 km) away. These jumps require troops to wear special helmets. The helmets are equipped with oxygen so the troops can breathe at high altitudes.

Underwater, special ops use rebreathers, a type of underwater diving equipment. The LAR-V MK25 is a closed-circuit system. This means the exhaled gas is returned to the tank using a hose. There the carbon dioxide is removed. This type of system doesn't create any bubbles, which would allow enemies to easily see a swimmer.

★★★★★
FACT

One member of SEAL Team Six carried the following on the Osama bin Laden raid: Sig Sauer P226 pistol, CamelBak hydration pack, energy gel shots, M4 rifle, field trauma kit to stop bleeding, and a noise canceling headset while on the Black Hawk.

SPECIAL OPS GEAR

L-3 GPNVG-18 GROUND PANORAMIC NIGHT VISION GOGGLES

COST: $65,000

TUBES: 4

WEIGHT: 27 ounces (765 grams)

WIDTH: 8.5 inches (21.6 cm)

FIELD OF VIEW: 97 degrees

LAR-V MK 25 REBREATHER

CAPACITY: about four hours of oxygen

WEIGHT: 27 to 31 pounds (12.2 to 14.1 kg) when full

LENGTH: about 18 inches (45.7 cm)

WIDTH: about 13 inches (33 cm)

HEIGHT: about 7 inches (17.8 cm)

RA-1 PARACHUTE

MAXIMUM JUMP HEIGHT: 35,000 feet (10,668 m)

COST: $10,000

MAIN PARACHUTE AREA: 360 square feet (33.4 square meters)

RANGE: a soldier can glide to a target 30 miles (47 km) from the transport aircraft

CAPACITY: can carry up to 450 pounds (204 kg)

★ ★ ★ ★ ★ ★ ★ ★ ☆

CHAPTER 7

SPECIAL OPS IN ACTION

Throughout history, special ops have used stealth, speed, and surprise to launch daring operations. During the Civil War, Confederate John Singleton Mosby commanded a special ops group known as Mosby's Rangers. The group attacked Northern troops across northern Virginia.

Confederate John Mosby questions soldiers from the North.

In one legendary raid, Mosby sneaked up on Northern General Edwin Stoughton at the Gunnell House on June 10, 1863. Creeping into the bedroom where the general slept, Mosby pulled down the sheets and slapped Stoughton on the behind. Mosby asked Stoughton, "Have you ever heard of Mosby?"

"Yes, have you caught him?" asked the general.

"No, but he has caught you," said Mosby, taking Stoughton prisoner. Mosby is sometimes considered the father of these kinds of surprise attacks.

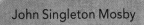

John Singleton Mosby

JUNE 10, 1863
the date Mosby's Rangers were established

1 the number of horses Mosby's men bought for him with money they stole from an Army paymaster during the Greenback Raid October 14, 1964

8 the number of companies Mosby's Rangers had at its height

15 the number of men originally assigned to Mosby

18 the average age of Mosby's Rangers. Some were only 14 or 15 years old.

29 the number of Rangers who sneaked into Stoughton's camp

33 the number of prisoners the Rangers took from Stoughton's camp

43 the number of Mosby's battalion, the 43rd Battalion Virginia Cavalry

58 the number of horses taken by the Rangers during the raid on Stoughton's camp

1,900 the number of men in Mosby's Rangers when the group was disbanded in April 1865

WILLIAM CUSHING: LINCOLN'S COMMANDO

William Cushing is known as "Lincoln's **Commando**." Some think of Cushing as the first Navy SEAL. Cushing used his ships to launch attacks on Confederate camps along the Virginia coast in 1862.

But Cushing's most daring act came in 1864. In October of that year, he sunk the Confederate ironclad USS *Albemarle*. The *Albemarle* was anchored on the Roanoke River in Plymouth, North Carolina. Floating logs surrounded the *Albemarle*. The logs were there to keep enemy boats from approaching. Cushing and his men sneaked up on a small boat. They sped over the floating logs. When the Confederates saw Cushing, they fired. Yet Cushing was able to slip a torpedo under the *Albemarle's* iron sides. When the torpedo exploded, the ship eventually sunk.

William Cushing and his crew blow up the *Albemarle*.

commando—a specially-trained soldier who makes quick, destructive raids on enemy territory

2 the number of boats Cushing used in the attack on the *Albemarle*. One was attacked by Confederates and sunk before it even reached the ironclad.

$20 the amount of money Cushing paid an old man to confirm that the *Albemarle* had sunk

13 the number of men Cushing took on his mission to destroy the *Albemarle*

4,000 the number of Confederate troops in the Plymouth area at the time of the attack

William Cushing

CSS *ALBEMARLE*

LENGTH: 125 feet (38.1 m)

SPEED: 5 knots (5.8 mph) (9.3 kmph)

WEIGHT: 376 tons (341 metric tons)

THICKNESS OF THE IRON SIDES: up to 4 inches (10.2 cm)

WEAPONS: two 6.4-inch (16.3-cm) double-banded rifled cannons and one ram made of iron and oak

MARINE CORPS RAIDERS AT GUADALCANAL

The Marine Corps created the Marine Raiders in February 1942 during World War II. One of the special ops group's most daring operations happened on the Pacific island of Guadalcanal.

 U.S. Marines comb the jungle looking for Japanese snipers during World War II.

malaria—a serious disease that people get from mosquito bites; malaria causes high fever, chills, and sometimes death

dysentery—a serious infection of the intestines that can be deadly; dysentery is often caused by drinking contaminated water

In November 1942 Marine Corps Raiders from the 2nd Battalion landed on the island. They were led by Lieutenant Colonel Evans Carlson. The Raiders' job was to secure a beach so Army soldiers, Seabees, and other Marines could land on the Japanese-controlled island. The plan was for the United States to build a new airfield in the area. With a regiment of Japanese moving through the jungle, the U.S. commanding general gave Carlson new orders. The Raiders were to harass the enemy. The Raiders spent a month surprising and attacking the Japanese during what became known as "The Long Patrol."

4 the number of days of food Carlson's Raiders carried. Later they received additional supplies of tea, rice, raisins, bacon, and sometimes chocolate.

16 the number of Raiders who died during the patrol

18 the number of Marines wounded during the operation

30 the number of days Carlson and his men spent behind Japanese lines

150 the length in miles (241 km) that Carlson and his Raiders covered during their patrol

225 the number of Raiders who became sick with **malaria**, **dysentery**, and ringworm during the operation

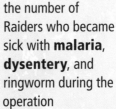

488 the number of Japanese the Raiders killed on Guadalcanal

OPERATION THURSDAY

U.S. Air Force special ops played an important role in Burma during World War II. Burma bordered China, which fought with the United States, and the British colony of India. Japan had invaded Burma in 1941, which was a threat to both India and China. To defeat the Japanese in Burma, the Allies planned to take British-led commandos into Burma aboard airplanes. They called this plan Operation Thursday. General Henry H. "Hap" Arnold led the aerial part of the invasion.

The operation began in March 1944. Arnold's group landed and built an airstrip. This allowed transport planes to land soldiers behind enemy lines. Cargo planes towing gliders delivered supplies.

Generals Henry Arnold (left) and Claire Chennault look at a Curtiss P-40 aircraft in 1943.

Though Operation Thursday lasted a week, Arnold's "Air Commandos" spent from late March until May delivering supplies to the ground troops. They evacuated injured soldiers using air ambulances. Meanwhile, bomber pilots communicated with commandos on the ground to hit enemy targets. These are all tasks of Air Force special ops today.

1 the number of days it took to build the airstrip

2 the number of months the Air Commandos supported ground troops in Burma

4 the number of soldiers rescued by Lieutenant Carter Harman during the first-ever wartime helicopter rescue in Burma

100 the number of flights flown to the airstrip the first night, about 10 per hour

175 the number of horses delivered during Operation Thursday

348 the number of aircraft planned for the operation. Aircraft included gliders, fighters, air ambulances, transports, bombers, and helicopters.

523 the number of men assigned to the air operation

1,283 the number of mules delivered during Operation Thursday

9,502 the number of troops flown into Burma during one week in March 1944

509,083 the weight in pounds (230,916 kg) of the supplies that landed during Operation Thursday

HOSTAGE RESCUE

In Afghanistan Green Berets work in places, such as Chamkani, where helicopters and big army vehicles can't reach. They train local police to help stop the enemy Taliban and meet with local leaders. Hiking miles through steep hills, Green Berets also surprise enemies moving weapons and fighters coming from nearby Pakistan.

On November 10, 2011, Army Special Forces soldiers rescued hostages inside a government building in Chamkani. U.S. soldiers and local leaders were meeting inside the building when enemies attacked. During the rescue Army Special Forces soldier Matthew Brown caught a grenade and tossed it away to save an Afghan soldier. Fellow Army Special Forces soldier Jason Myers fought his way into the building three times during the night and was seriously injured.

U.S. Special Forces and Afghan commandos provide security for villagers in Afghanistan.

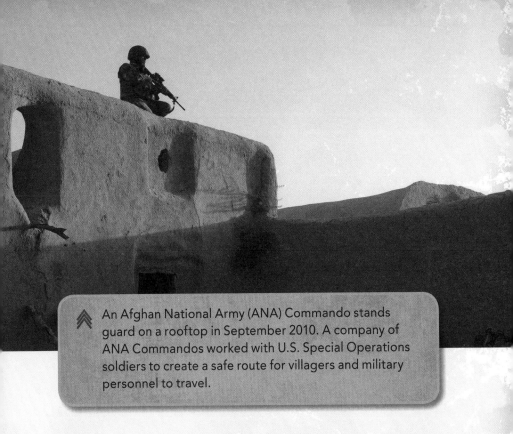

An Afghan National Army (ANA) Commando stands guard on a rooftop in September 2010. A company of ANA Commandos worked with U.S. Special Operations soldiers to create a safe route for villagers and military personnel to travel.

2 the number of Afghan leaders taken hostage during the attack

2 the number of Army Special Forces soldiers who came to the rescue, along with three Afghans

3 the number of Afghan police the enemies killed

5 the number of medals two Army Special Forces soldiers earned for their rescue

5 TO 10 the number of enemies, some armed with grenades, vests with bombs, and automatic weapons

12 the number of Army Special Forces soldiers typically at the Chamkani base along with a small number of other army troops

OSAMA BIN LADEN MISSION

Early in the morning on May 2, 2011, U.S. Navy SEALs loaded their guns before landing at a compound in Pakistan. One of America's worst enemies was inside. Osama bin Laden had planned the September 11, 2001, terrorist attacks that killed about 3,000 people in the United States. Now an Air Force **drone** flew above the compound. It sent video of the mission to the U.S. president.

SEALs fought their way into the house and killed bin Laden. Then they took bin Laden's computer files. The files revealed terrorist plots including that bin Laden wanted to kill President Barack Obama. The SEALS and Night Stalkers involved in the raid had possibly saved many lives.

People gather outside Osama bin Laden's compound after he was killed.

1 the number of dogs aboard the helicopters. A Belgian Malinois named Cairo helped keep an eye on the outside of the house. If needed, Cairo could find false doors and secret rooms inside the house.

2

the number of MH-60 Black Hawk helicopters piloted be Night Stalkers that delivered the SEALs to their target

6 the number of the SEAL team that carried out the mission

23 the number of SEALs involved in the mission—12 in the first helicopter and 11 in the second

90 the number of minutes the helicopter flight took from Jalalabad Air Field in eastern Afghanistan to bin Laden's compound

15,000 the height in feet (4,572 m) that the RQ-170 drone flew over the compound during the operation

9 YEARS, **7** MONTHS, AND **20** DAYS the amount of time between the September 11 terrorist attacks and bin Laden's death

drone—an unmanned, remote-controlled aircraft

★ ★ ★ ★ ★ ★ ★ ★ ★

CHAPTER 8

FIGHTING TOGETHER

Today U.S. special ops groups work together around the globe. The U.S. Special Operations Command coordinates all U.S. special ops. It includes each military branch's special ops. This includes operators such as SEALs and Green Berets. It also involves all the teams who support the missions, such as supply and communications personnel.

 Members of the Joint Special Operations Task Force give medical aid to a man in Afghanistan.

One part of U.S. Special Operations Command is the Joint Special Operations Command (JSOC). JSOC carries out missions using operators from various services, including Delta Force, SEALs, Rangers, Air Force Special Tactics, and the Night Stalkers. JSOC operates its own intelligence, drones, and satellites. It planned the Osama bin Laden raid. JSOC often conducts raids to gather information. Then it **analyzes** the information and targets other terrorists.

Special ops fighters are unique. Each service selects only the best. Then they are put though intense training. Only the strongest serve.

JSOC STATS

20 the estimated number of minutes it takes the JSOC to analyze information from a raid and target other terrorists

80 the number of countries the JSOC operates in, including Iraq, Afghanistan, Yemen, Pakistan, Somalia, Nigeria, and the Philippines

1980 the year the JSOC was founded as an anti-terrorism unit

1,800 the number of people in the JSOC before the 9/11 terrorist attacks. This includes operators and support staff.

25,000 the number of people working in JSOC in 2011

analyze—to examine something carefully in order to understand it

agent (AY-juhnt)—a spy

analyze (AN-uh-lize)—to examine something carefully in order to understand it

battalion (buh-TAL-yuhn)—a group of about 300 to 1,000 soldiers

commando (kuh-MAN-doh)—a specially-trained soldier who makes quick, destructive raids on enemy territory

demolition (de-muh-LI-shuhn)—the act of destroying something

drone (DROHN)—an unmanned, remote-controlled aircraft

dysentery (DI-sen-tayr-ee)—a serious infection of the intestines that can be deadly; dysentery is often caused by drinking contaminated water

elite (i-LEET)—among the very best

hostage (HOSS-tij)—a person held against his or her will

intelligence (in-TEL-uh-jenss)—secret information about an enemy's plans or actions

malaria (muh-LAIR-ee-ah)—a serious disease that people get from mosquito bites; malaria causes high fever, chills, and sometimes death

raid (RAYD)—a sudden, surprise attack on a place

resistance (ri-ZISS-tuhnss)—a group that fights back against those in control of a conquered country; resistance members often operate in secret

squadron (SKWAHD-ruhn)—the basic fighting unit of the U.S. Air Force

suppressor (suh-PRESS-er)—a device on the barrel of a gun that reduces the noise when the gun is fired

tactic (TAK-tik)—a plan for fighting a battle

terrorist (TAYR-ur-ist)—someone who uses violence and threats to frighten people

READ MORE

Bolt, Lisa M. *U.S. Army Green Berets: A Timline.* Special Ops Mission Timelines. North Mankato, Minn.: Capstone Press, 2016.

Gregory, Josh. *Special Ops.* Cool Military Careers. Ann Arbor, Mich.: Cherry Lake Publishing, 2013.

Stillwell, Alexander. *Marines: What It Takes to Join the Elite.* Military Jobs. New York: Cavendish Square, 2015.

INTERNET SITES

FactHound offers a safe, fun way to find Internet sites related to this book. All of the sites on FactHound have been researched by our staff.

Here's all you do:
Visit *www.facthound.com*
Type in this code: 9781515718529

CRITICAL THINKING USING THE COMMON CORE

1. How have new technologies changed Special Operations? (Key Ideas and Details)

2. Why have special ops become so important in today's military? (Integration of Knowledge and Ideas)

3. What traits do special ops personnel need to do their jobs? (Integration of Knowledge and Ideas)